Reinelt

Magic
of
Character Dolls

Sabine Reinelt

Magic
of
Character Dolls

Images of Children

English Translation by Lydia Pauli, M.D.

Published by · Hobby House Press · Grantsville, Maryland 21536

Additional copies of this book may be purchased at $29.95
from
HOBBY HOUSE PRESS, INC.
1 Corporate Drive
Grantsville, Maryland 21536
Or Call 1-800-554-1447

or from your favorite bookstore or dealer.
Please add $5.50 per copy for postage.

Table of Contents

Dolls that Look Like Children — Sculptured Snapshots

For many years in the evenings, when my children finally fall asleep, I reflect upon my dolls, and for a while I fall under the spell of their pensive, joyful, pouting or dreamy expressions, and each time I ask myself again why do they have such a hold on me.

It is a feeling of an unchangeable moment of an expression on a child's face that passes fleetingly. I dream back with my dolls who are guarding me against what slips by so fast in my everyday life.

Almost every doll charms me. I would love to have many of them. But in view of today's prices and the rarity of some of the dolls, this is not possible.

So evolved a need to capture with a camera the many little individuals I saw in my friends' collections for myself and those who share my feelings.

I was interested more in the doll children, less in the babies and young ladies. The babies are touching and sweet. But it is the children that are full of thoughts, actions, self-confidence and life. It is this life which I see in them that I like to express with my pictures. They show children in situations and surroundings suited to their mood expressions. This book is not intended to be a textbook, but rather a pleasure for lay people and collectors alike. However, I believe that even the experienced collector will find something unusual and surprising. The Kämmer & Reinhardt 115A with open mouth was never before shown. The 116A was unknown as a black child. I would especially like to show the singular beauty of some of the very rare dolls of Hertel, Schwab & Co., Baehr & Proeschild and Kestner to counterbalance the one-sided search for the standard type of the Kämmer & Reinhardt series. But I cannot find it in my heart to leave these out, even though they have been pictured so many times. Their faces are too charming for me to resist. Without any doubt they belong here.

The character dolls should really be called artist dolls since they are creations by artists who preserved their innate magic for all times. They should be the children's best playmates for they resemble them the most. This is the reason they were made. But for us adults they became a great gift — they are images of children.

Sabine Reinelt

The Variable History of Character Dolls

"Not dolls — they should be called real children" — so wrote a newspaper in 1912 about the artist dolls whose appearance in 1908 in Munich signaled the beginning of the doll reform.

The story of the character dolls was stormy. Though basically artist dolls, they were called "character dolls" based on the head with "a meaningful, sometimes distinct characterization" (Franz Reinhardt). Thanks to the various expressions of the faces, more than other dolls they aroused great raptures and rabid rejection, even condemnation. But the spirits took their revenge, today, seventy years after they were destroyed in thousands, they are among the most loved and sought after dolls!

The special charm of the character dolls is in their portrayal of real children and not the idealized, expressionless perfect beauty. These children express defiance, joy, grief, thoughtfulness, laughter and tears. These little ingenious sculptures evoke feelings from the observer. Who would not want to embrace and comfort a sad child? Who would not be infected by a child's laughter? Obviously, the artists who created the character dolls and the companies that manufactured them, all wanted to give children dolls that could draw out a feeling of affection, care, comfort. They wanted to get away from the ever perfect, accomplished, expressionless exterior of the "beautiful doll". They wanted a child for a child, which would awaken emotions; they wanted a little girl to feel like a mother, not like a child needing improvement, who could never measure up to their faultless doll.

But the new enthusiasm for the unadulterated childlikeness, the charm of a defiant little obstinate child or a pouting child, did not last. The children were still nice, but should one, was one allowed to give them dolls that were so capricious? Shouldn't they have dolls with a noncommittal expression, so that they could play

various roles, today a nurse and tomorrow a child in kindergarten? While the discussions about the "correct" doll expression became heated, other events influenced their further development. For a time, both the German and the Unified French Companies (SFBJ) were all in favor of producing character dolls. But they soon recognized that the "Prettyfied" modest character child, mostly baby dolls, had the best selling potential. The war and the inflation following made necessary a more simplified production.

The unbelievable variety of character dolls produced between 1909 and 1914 disappeared overnight. The Americans, who benefited financially from the German inflation, bought out the remainder of the German doll production at ridiculously low prices. After the German

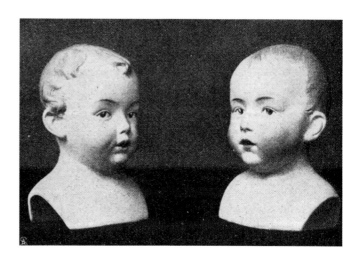

"Two new doll heads; though they cannot be described as 'character' heads they do not show the lifeless stare characteristic of the previous porcelain dolls. They will probably find more approval from small children than the 'artistic' dolls, for which the taste of our young and the children is not yet ripe", such was the contemporary description. To us it is obvious that the modeling is that of character heads. In 1911 such name was given only to dolls with pronounced individual characteristics.

Character children.

One can almost hear a loud roar when one looks at this doll. She is marked only Germany 3, by Gebräder Heubach, 15¾in (40cm) high, circa 1914.

monetary reform, when the "Rentenmark" no longer allowed such a favorable exchange, the American demand for the porcelain dolls stopped abruptly. Many German factories had closed. For them the period of the character dolls was just a lively interlude. The golden age of the character dolls lasted only five years (except for some models produced in the twenties). An unbelievable profusion of vastly different, strong expressive types was produced in that brief time. For example in 1909 Kämmer & Reinhardt, alone, introduced 15 various doll models and 16 additional models until 1914. Another even more perplexing variety of various heads (among them many extreme heads) was created by the Gebrüder Heubach Company. This firm must have produced hundreds of different character types. The Gebrüder Heubach was subsequently the only remaining company producing character dolls until they closed in 1938. Even today there appear occasionally whole lots of Heubach character heads. It is nearly impossible to imagine the activity of the German companies in those few years and the enterprising spirit that made it possible to bring ever newer dolls to the market. Thus today's collector encounters such a vast multitude of the character dolls that it seems they were the production of several decades. Some of these beloved character dolls were produced in very small numbers. On the other hand many, for instance baby "100" by Kämmer & Reinhardt, some by Heubach, but especially the gentle character baby with head mark 126 by Kämmer & Reinhardt were produced in masses.

Despite all the enthusiasm for collecting character dolls, the attention was limited to a few types. There were several reasons: one collected what was known, what was admired liked in a friend's home, what was pictured in a book or what was generally available. This lead to a difference in values and with that to increased prices in some companies, while many really charming dolls, since not generally known, remained unnoticed. With the great demand for Kämmer & Reinhardt dolls, even though some of the series were not very rare, the prices raised incredibly.

There is no doubt that the "children" from Kämmer & Reinhardt belong to the most beautiful dolls produced at that time. There is a good reason for the intensity of their expression. Only recently the mystery of their creation was discovered. The famous Berlin sculptor, Arthur Lewin-Funke (1866-1937), who received many prizes, probably modeled all the series from 100 to 112. (Three models from this Series 108, 110 and 111 were either not produced or are missing). It seems quite sure that the 101 and some other models (for instance 103, 104, 105 and possibly 112) are the images of his first born daughter, Karin, born in 1904. These are sculptures of a recognized artist which he created with a great

personal affection. It is not surprising that they touch us to this day. In his time it would have been a disadvantage if it had been known that a serious and famous artist modelled doll's faces. Thus the cooperation between the two partners Lewin-Funke and Franz Reinhardt was kept secret. From the series 114 on the doll heads were created by the modeller from the firm of Karl Krausser. Fortunately there were also other companies who created singularly strong expressive faces.

It is the desire of this author to show dolls which were overlooked until now or dolls that were unknown. Unfortunately, some of them are extremely rare. The character children were the passion of adults. The children desired babies and so the character doll surge finally ended where it began. In the beginning a baby doll was created and with the passage of time there was an ever increasing demand for the baby types and eventually they became the main theme of the doll production. In spite of this the variety of character types is just unbelievable. Long before 1909 there existed some distinct character faces, for example those by

The modeller Karl Krausser working for Kämmer & Reinhardt designed this doll, Hans or Gretchen (series number 114) after the grandchild of Franz Reinhardt.

The child and her doll, she searches for something of herself in her small playmate. Before the doll reform she should have recognized the type in the doll ("Hidden Teacher"). The character doll on the other hand should help her to identify through recognition and understanding.

Walter, series number 102 belongs to the rare members of the character family. Jointed body, 11¾in (30cm) high, circa 1909.

Simon & Halbig and Jumeau. One can only assume that the adults found it exciting to capture in always newer forms the magic of the children's faces.

I do not find the present enthusiasm for character dolls a fad. It is a joy in creating and with it preserving that something which catches the magic of a child's face. It is not surprising then that the character dolls represented a smaller part of the production. It could not succeed for an extended time and many were even destroyed. They were in my eyes not only dolls but small works of art. There were other dolls to play with, Käthe Kruse dolls, baby dolls, celluloid dolls and others more suitable for playing. The character doll does not come to life by being played with, it represents a part of life.

Whistling Jim. One of the most famous character dolls by Gebrüder Heubach originated around 1914. Signature 8774, 10½in (27cm) high, original clothes.

This charming youngster with an engaging smile has only mark I. Jointed body, expression is similar to the dolls made by Hertel, Schwab & Co. and Baehr & Proeschild. 12½ in (32 cm) high.

Peter

Marie

Marie (101), porcelain image of
a child picking strawberries.
17in (43 cm)

Hans

Gretchen

It now seems certain: "Marie," Model 101 was modelled on a child. Arthur Lewin-Funke, the renown Berlin artist, modelled his almost four year old daughter, Karin. From this came the Series 101. She later served as model for 103, 104 and 105 and possibly for 112. The Series 114 was modelled by Karl Krausser for Kämmer & Reinhardt and was modelled from live children.

The expressions of these children images are most beautiful when a "snapshot of the moment" is associated with some kind of activity.   When Max no longer stands in the open with a silent grin, but slyly slips through the neighbor's garden fence and swipes an apple. When Moritz scratches the ear of a stone figure. When Peter rolls his eyes at Marie and a sitting young lady collects flowers.

And so I started to photograph them because I had an irresistible desire to show these dolls in all their vivacity. In photographing them I fell in love with each doll all over again.

Dolls by Baehr & Proeschild:
The Angry Indian
and the Charming Children

Charming girl with head mark
604 from the firm Baehr &
Proeschild, toddler type body,
16½in (42cm), circa 1920.

This girl, also by Baehr & Proeschild, is marked number 2072. It was created in the twenties and belongs in the series of character dolls which were made for the firm of Bruno Schmidt, Waltershausen. Toddler type body, 19½in (50cm) high.

This Indian is marked 244 with no other company identification. The wigged closed head shows an indentation under the wig with a hole for fastening of elastic loops. The eyes are not movable. The inside of the front half of the face is fully plastered. He has simple brown body with straight arms and legs and molded shoes. Made by Baehr & Proeschild, 16½in (42cm), original clothes.

Baehr & Proeschild made many dolls for Bruno Schmidt. This girl shows quite a remarkable resemblance to the doll in Series No. 536. She is marked with 2025-54 (for the size), BSW in heart and number 529. The same doll comes also signed BP and 529. Circa 1912.

A quiet friendly smiling doll with painted eyes is marked only 536. She was cast by Baehr & Proeschild in 1912. This doll is sometimes found with B.P. and heart mark. Jointed body. 16½in (42cm).

Little Wendy takes care of her little doll in a Marklin baby carriage. 2033, BSW 537, jointed body, straight wrists.

"The Little Doll Mothers"

Heinrich Handwerck

This doll with head mark 119 designed by Heinrich Handwerck was contracted to Simon & Halbig. As a gypsy she is rare and especially charming. Jointed body, 17½in (45cm), circa 1900.

Ernst Heubach:
Lofty Girls and Little Rascals

A black girl with large eyes. She is form Series 344. Jointed, 17½in (45cm) high. Circa 1920s.

This enterprising boy was made by Ernst Heubach. He is marked E.H. 262/1, very rare. Jointed body, 8½ in (22 cm), circa 1914.

Gebrüder Heubach:
Children Dolls Who Laugh,
Cry, Whistle or Dream

This doll's only head mark is 7 1/2 DEP. A very similar doll has the head mark 5636. They belong in the group of "smiling babies." 20½in (52cm) high, circa 1912.

The variety of the types of the character dolls by Gebrüder Heubach seems unsurpassed. The doll with Series Number 6969, though not extremely rare, is especially beautiful. She has large painted eyes and is dressed in an attractive old Siebenbuergen regional costume. 13½in (34cm) high.

A dreaming child with number
7075 made by Gebrüder
Heubach around 1912. Jointed
body, 18½in (47cm) high.

A cunning Heubach character with head mark 8548, painted eyes, molded hair, baby body, 23½in (60cm) high, circa 1912.

This doll presumably number 7407 by Gebrüder Heubach is of particularly good quality. The Heubach dolls vary greatly in the execution. This doll also came in a lesser quality. Jointed body, 18½in (47cm) high, circa 1912.

This well-bred boy from a good family with painted eyes has an especially well formed mouth. He is marked number 7622, jointed body, 17½in (45cm) high, circa 1912.

Previously unknown black boy with a strongly modelled expression was made by Gebrüder Heubach. Signed 7668, jointed body, 15½in (39cm) high, circa 1912.

27

A small molded line in the lower lip gives this face an especially touching expression. This doll with head mark 8420, though not the rarest, belongs to the most beautiful Heubach models. This little doll has a baby body, 11in (28cm) high. A larger doll has a toddler body, is 16½in (42cm) high. Circa 1914.

The number "9570" with a transverse number 8 underneath is the only mark on this doll. She belongs to the Gebrüder Heubach number system even though the modelling is not typical. Jointed body, 17½in (45cm), old clothing.

Hertel, Schwab & Co.:
Creators of Dreamlike Dolls

The firm Hertel, Schwab & Co., Stutzhaus, produced dolls of exceptional quality. Because they were marked only with a number, they were often falsely attributed to Kestner. Some of the dolls of the 100 series appeared to have been made to order for Kley & Hahn, but not this model marked 134, which is extremely rare. Jointed body, old clothing, 15¾in (40cm), circa 1912.

Outstanding porcelain and a perfect peaceful expression characterize this rare doll, made by Hertel, Schwab & Co. after their own design. Head mark 141, jointed body, old clothing, 25in (64cm), circa 1912.

This doll with the head mark 149 belongs to the most beautiful dolls made by Hertel, Schwab & Co. The smaller sizes were often on baby bodies, the larger ones on jointed bodies. She was made with painted and sleep eyes, jointed body, 15¾in (40cm), circa 1912.

This doll is an enigma: she has series number "154" and was most likely produced by Hertel, Schwab & Co. for Kley & Hahn. A doll of almost the same shape, occasionally called Tommy Tucker, with an open mouth and series number 2048 and 2096 by Baehr & Proeschild was made for Bruno Schmidt. The pictured doll has closed mouth, toddler body, 21in (53cm), circa 1912.

Doll marked Kley & Hahn number 169-1 was made by Hertel, Schwab & Co. Closed mouth (some with an open mouth), baby body, 11in (28cm), circa 1912.

Kämmer & Reinhardt Designs: Lifelike Children

This series of character dolls was started with the famous baby of Kämmer & Reinhardt number 100. This baby comes in white (frequent), brown (rarer), Oriental (very rare) and with wig and glass sleep eyes (also very rare). This picture shows a baby in a Marklin wheelbarrow, being photographed by his brother "Phillip" with head mark number 115A, 23in (53cm) high. The baby was produced from 1909, the 115 from 1911.

Delicate flirting between Marie, number 101, 17in (43cm), and Hans, 114, 18in (46cm).

Exquisite, rare, brown Marie, number 101, jointed body, original dress, 17in (43cm).

Karl, series number 107, is also
rare. This one is particularly
handsome. Jointed body, 21½in
(55cm) high, circa 1909.

This doll number 112 has glass eyes and toddler type body. old clothing, 15¾in (40cm) high.

This boy, number 112 exudes vivacity. This doll came with baby body, jointed or toddler type body. 15¾in (40cm), circa 1910.

Elsie, series number 109, jointed body, 19¼in (49cm) high, circa 1909.

This extremely rare doll with head mark number 103 by Kämmer & Reinhardt can be admired in the doll collection of Legoland, Billund (Denmark). Jointed body, 23in (58cm), circa 1909.

During the week this little one, number 112, works in a confectioner's store. Kämmer & Reinhardt, painted eyes, smaller jointed body, original dress, 7in (19cm).

On weekends she and her larger sister Grete collect mushrooms. Grete, number 114, Kämmer & Reinhardt, painted eyes, jointed body, old clothing, 13½in (34cm).

Cinderella, a small number 114
with glass eyes, jointed body,
11¾ (30cm), she has to pick up
lentils...

.... while her sister is allowed to play piano, number 114, with brown painted eyes, jointed body, 15½ (39cm), circa 1909.

Even if Kämmer & Reinhardt never made another doll, they would have been famous with this number 114 doll. Blue glass eyes, jointed body 18in (46cm) high, circa 1911.

This little doll pushes a Marklin sled. She is number 115A, toddler type body, closed mouth, 11¾in (30cm) high.

If anybody thought that the character series by Kämmer & Reinhardt could not offer any more surprises, he would have been mistaken. Though she was mentioned in a book on markings, nobody so far took notice of this number 115A with open mouth, possibly there were only a few samples. Glass sleep eyes, 11¾in (30cm) high.

Hanschen in a blueberry field with head mark number 116A. This friendly doll came as a baby doll and very rarely as a small child with toddler body. She was available with open and closed mouth. This doll has an open mouth with a glued on cardboard inside, toddler body, old clothing, 12½in (32cm) high, circa 1911.

This number 116A as a black
child, charming curiousity,
toddler type body, 15½in
(39cm) high, circa 1912.

This number 116A has a jointed
body (hip ball joint, no disc joint
as in a toddler body). All
original condition, great dark
brown eyes, 19½in (50cm).

Number 117A radiates charm
but not all of this series possess
so much sweetness. Brown glass
sleep eyes, jointed body, old
clothing, 24½in (62cm) high.

Picture pretty number 117 and she knows it! Jointed body, 23in (58cm), circa 1911.

This number 117, with gray-blue glass sleep eyes, jointed body, plays a doll harp. Original dress, 17 in (43 cm).

This doll with series number 120 is from the same mold as her sister in the 117 series with closed mouth, not the number 117 which has a different face mold. The number "120" is quite a rare doll. Glass sleep eyes, jointed body, original dress, 19½in (50cm), circa 1915.

The doll with the series number 121 resembles greatly the 118 and the 122, all dainty, lively girl types. Blue glass sleep eyes, dimples, toddler type body with fixed wrists. Original dress, 19½in (50cm) high, circa 1912.

This doll in series number 122 flirts incredulously because of her specially outwards turned roguish sleep eyes. Toddler body, 15¾in (40cm) high, circa 1912.

The "Googly" also belongs in the character series of Kämmer & Reinhardt. An innovation that started in America and was taken over by German companies, the dolls have so called crossed eyes, and strong grinning watermelon style mouth. The hands are spread like the Kewpie dolls. This rare doll is marked series number 131,24 (for the body size), but in reality she is 1in (3cm) higher. Straight modelled arms and legs. Original condition, circa 1914.

The famous siblings pair Max and Moritz from Wilhelm Busch inspired many doll manufacturers, for example, Kämmer & Reinhardt, Kestner, Schildkröt and Juno. It is difficult to know whether they were really popular with children. I was told by one owner that the dolls were kept mostly in the closet. The dolls from the Kämmer and Reinhardt character series are especially well modelled and very lovable. Regrettably, they are quite rare because they were unsuitable play dolls. Both dolls have glass sleep eyes with a sidewise turning mechanism, jointed bodies with straight wrists and modelled shoes. Max, series number 123, is 15¾in (40cm) high and was made in 1913.

Moritz, series number 124, is also 15¾in (40cm) high and has the same eye mechanism and body. His mouth is pulled slightly more up, while his brother Max has a wider grin. He was made at the same time as Max.

Kestner:
Lovable Round Faced Children

Kestner siblings with series number 179, 183 and 185. Description on page 60.

The familiar characteristics of the Kestner character dolls are demonstrated in this youngster with head mark 186. They have well nourished, friendly faces with a hint of white outlines under the eyes, short painted upper eyelashes in painted eyes (with glass eyes the eyelashes are painted on both upper and lower eyelids). This doll is only known with painted eyes. Jointed body, 13¾in (35cm), circa 1910.

The brown eyed boy with a dreaming expression has series number 179. The girl marked number 183 shows a hairstyle common in Kestner character dolls: the famous "German" plaits. Both dolls have jointed bodies. They were also made with glass eyes, 15¾in (40cm) high, circa 1910.

This nice smiling child has number 185. It was also made with glass eyes. Closed mouth, blue painted eyes, jointed body, 15¾in (40cm) high, circa 1910.

This doll has a decidedly friendly face. Series number 187. Jointed body, 19in (48cm) high, circa 1910.

The owner named this doll "Friederike." Series number 182, brown painted eyes, smiling closed mouth, jointed body, 14½in (37cm) high, circa 1910

This rare doll with head mark
206 has a typical round face,
suggestive eye outline and an
especially striking heart shaped
mouth. Only dolls with glass
eyes are known in this series.
Jointed body, 19in (48cm), circa
1911.

This little boy was marked J.D.K. 211. Starting from this number on the Kestner Company made these dolls recognizable and it is not a problem for today's collectors. Jointed body, 12½in (32cm) high, circa 1912.

Hilda, here with the head mark 237/1070 comes usually with a baby body. She is especially desirable with a toddler body. 15¾in (40cm) high. This trademark was entered in 1914.

Koenig & Wernicke

This doll was brought to market with series number 1070 by Koenig & Wernicke. She is made of very luminous fine porcelain. This is not surprising since the firm was supplied with outstanding porcelain head manufactured by such companies as Hertel, Schwab & Co., Baeher & Proeschild and Armand Marseille. Open mouth, with two teeth, jointed body, 15¾in (40cm) high, circa 1915.

Armand Marseille:
Cheerful Playmates

The proud owner of the bear is this Armand Marseille googly with head mark 323. This sweet doll is not as rare as the Kämmer & Reinhardt googly, 8in (20cm), circa 1912.

This is a very rare doll by Armand Marseille, marked only with number 233. There is a doll also marked 233 which comes with a full A.M. mark. She has an astonished facial expression, open mouth, baby type body, 13¾in (35cm) high, circa 1920s.

This little character boy named "Kiddiejoy" from Armand Marseille is marked with series number 345. Simple body with straight arms and legs, 8½ in (22cm) high, circa 1913

Armand Marseille created character dolls of very high quality with bewitching expressions. This youngster, belonging to series 550, is made of an especially fine porcelain, jointed body, 15¾in (40cm) high, circa 1910.

The beloved "Fany" from Armand Marseille is known for her resemblance to Kämmer & Reinhardt number 115A doll. Both dolls and many other similar types are supposedly based on the model of a child's head by "Fiamingo" (a Dutch sculptor named Francois Duquesnois, who lived from 1594 to 1646). Kathe Kruse also used this as a model for her Doll Model I. Fany is differentiated from Kämmer & Reinhardt doll by the shape of her mouth. The lower lip is smaller. Both dolls have round toddler bodies with fixed wrists. Fany's thighs are not jointed with discs but rather with ball joints like in the jointed bodies. Head mark 231, 13¾in (35cm) high, registered trademark since 1912.

Open closed mouth smiles friendly, dimples: a small doll with series number 590, jointed body, old clothing, 13½in (34cm) high.

This cheerful girl is made from an especially good and smooth porcelain. Series number 590, jointed body with straight wrists, 15¾in (40cm) high.

Franz Schmidt & Co.

This doll has no company mark. The lively boy with unusually thick molded hair was introduced around 1912 by Franz Schmidt & Co. The doll has a jointed body and is 19½in (50cm) high.

Schoenau & Hoffmeister

This baby was made in the porcelain factory of Schoenau & Hoffmeister in Burggrub. She is signed with S, PB in star, H and letters KBH.   Sitting baby body with movable wrists, 15¾in (40cm), circa 1912.

Simon & Halbig:
The Company that Created Collector's Dreams

Although one could argue whether these dolls belong to the character dolls, the colorful Simon & Halbig dolls are without a doubt especially charming. This Oriental girl with series number 1029 belongs to the most exotic models. She wears an original dress, jointed body, 16½in (42cm) high. Presumably she was designed around 1890.

The doll with series number 1329 is occasionally called Burmese. However, she could as well be a child from India as is seen in these pictured dolls. The girl has a yellowish jointed body, 17in (45cm). She was manufactured circa 1910. Her brother is made of a lighter shade of porcelain. 15¾in (40cm) high.

Charming and very rare is this black child with series number 1368. Almond like fixed eyes, typical of Simon & Halbig. The Negroid traits are slightly less pronounced than in the 1358 series. Jointed body, old clothing, 13¾in (35cm) high, circa 1911.

This mulatto girl (series 1358) is holding a little baby, 16½in (42 cm) high.

This pair from series 1358 belongs to the most beautifully colored dolls. The dolls in this series vary in color from the café au lait to the deepest chocolate brown. The colors of the bodies are color coordinated. The pictured smaller doll is lighter, 16½in (42cm) high. The larger doll is darker, 19in (48cm) high. Both dolls have jointed bodies. The larger one wears an old silk dress. They were made circa 1910.

Right: "The Most Beautiful":
1448 with immaculate porcelain
of the highest quality, brown
glass sleep eyes, feathered
eyebrows and a seductive "kiss
mouth." Old clothing, jointed
body, 29in (74cm), circa 1914.

This neat youngster with an upturned nose is not easy to find. He has series number 1488, open closed mouth, jointed body, old clothing, 15¾in (40cm) high. Supposedly was still produced in the twenties.

This extremely rare doll with painted eyes and closed mouth from the series 150 from Simon & Halbig resembles greatly the series 107 from Kämmer & Reinhardt and Simon & Halbig. Perhaps the same child served as a model. Certainly there is the same model type in both dolls. The original dress for this doll was made after the convent school dress worn by the child owner of this doll. Jointed body, 15½ (39cm) high, circa 1912.

Erica is the name of this doll with series number 1489. She is also hard to find, and if found, is usually a baby. The pictured doll is rather a young lady with a jointed body. She is an "Ingrid Bergmann" type. 19in (50cm), circa 1920s.

Société Française de Fabrication de Bébés et Jouets: The Willful Little French Children

Automata dolls from the SFBJ character series: the legs can be moved by turning the head. The youngster has series number 227, his girlfriend is 236 (plentiful). Simple bodies with straight arms and legs, 11¾in (30cm) high, circa 1911.

The paperweight eyes beam joyfully in the brown face of this doll with series number 226 from the French companies syndicate SFBJ. This type comes as an European or as a Negro. The pictured doll is 12½in (32cm) high and wears an original dress. The hair is "flocked", i.e. hair that is very thick is cut short and is glued directly on the closed head. German companies, for instance Kämmer & Reinhardt and Gebrüder Heubach, used such a hairstyle occasionally. The series 226 mirrors the influence of the character babies number 100 from Kämmer & Reinhardt. In the subsequent models the French broke away from the German patterns and created French particularly quite willful faces. Signed SFBJ, 226, Paris, 4. Circa 1910.

This joyful child with number
238 is relatively rare. Fixed
paperweight eyes, jointed body,
15in (40cm) high, circa 1914.

This model with number 250 is almost unknown. The porcelain has a stronger tint which suggests that she was not made until the twenties. She has a jointed body and is 20½in (52cm) high.

The most interesting doll from the character line of S.F.B.J. has the series number 252. This rare doll is also called "Boudeur" and served as a model for the "Pouty" dolls with a distinct pouty mouth. Also unusual is the projection of the forehead. This doll is really stubborn. The pictured dolls have jointed bodies (this doll comes also as a baby), wear old clothing, 18in (46cm) high, circa 1920s.

Wagner & Zetzsche:
The Company Owner's
Children Preserved in Doll Form

In 1916 Wagner & Zetzsche Company bought a patent for manufacture of an unbreakable burnable material. They called it "Haralit" and the company immediately produced two doll heads for the market. Two of the Zetzsche's children, Harald and Inge, served as models for the first models. Later followed "Hansi" modeled after another Zetzsche's child. The few examples of these dolls that surface today are very strikingly light. It seems that the paint did not adhere too well to the new material. The body of this doll has jointed arms, the torso and the legs are made from artificial leather. marked Harald W.Z., 13¾in (35cm) high, circa 1916.

Beauty of Unknown Origin

It is not known so far who made this unknown beauty number 111. Occasionally she was thought to be the missing 111 from the Kämmer & Reinhardt's character series. However from the type characteristics she belongs to another series. This doll is very rare. The pictured doll has sleep eyes with eyelashes, jointed body, all original, 18in (46cm) high.

"Doll's Lullaby"

The tiny googly pair is un-
marked. Original dress, only
6in (15cm) high.

A pair of googlies of unknown
origin, shows only series
number 241, 11in (28cm) high.

The Character Doll:
The Conflict of Opinions
Between 1910 and 1914

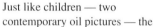

Just like children — two contemporary oil pictures — the character dolls were allowed to look dreaming or defiant.

"The dolls — the old lovely dolls — they have no longer doll faces — they look like people faces. As long as the world existed, all dolls looked alike. They were made of wood and some from leather, there were dolls with real human hair or bald dolls, there were big dolls and little dolls, there were dolls that cried, 'Papa-Mama' and such that could be squeezed without shattering the ears, but all the dolls had the same fixed look, the same unbelievably healthy color, the same facial expression, and if one may say so, their expression was doll-like, devoid of expression.

"They looked like the governesses thought exemplary children should look: well mannered, well tanned, pink and dull. Generations of growing girls could take an example from them. But they did not. Defying the governesses, suddenly they developed their own minds. This was bad enough. But now, long after the girls started to feel like individuals and personalities they all of a sudden started to imitate their dolls. This is without doubt a sign of a near world collapse.

"Next Christmas Lieschen will find a new character doll under the tree. Her old common doll lost her arm. The new character doll has pretty, interesting hands. She looks very good. Just like a child, real child, not like a

governess's model child. She has dimples. The little nose looks a little pointed. The eyes look defiant. Now when Lieschen plays mamma, she can educate her doll who looks like she is in need of education (the old doll was always so very good and the little mother often not at all). This is all good but what happens when Lieschen does not want to play mamma but to play a company visit? Did one ever see a lady who comes to visit who has a pointed little nose and looks defiant? Or can a character doll represent a fairy? The old doll with the missing arm could be all these people. She did not look like anybody — thus like everybody..."

To be sure, we grown-ups take a pleasure in well made creatures. Only, I think, we should not be embarrassed and we should play with them openly. (From the *Berliner Tagblatt*, September 15, 1910.)

"Actually a doll should not be a lady, not a lace covered being in a delicate silk dress, it should represent a child, a being that looks outwardly just like a child, that can awaken an illusion in the heart of the little mother: this is your child a doll child that can be protected and watched over.

Albert Schoenhut, an American, whose family of woodcarvers emigrated from Württenberg also brought character dolls to the market in 1911. They were made entirely from wood, from the carved hair to the toes, and had painted eyes. Later on he added wigs and even later glass eyes. An early Schoenhut doll with easy movable wooden jointed body (the feet too have joints and a hole in the sole so that the doll can stand on its own), molded hair, 15in (38cm), circa 1911.

"The impression the usual doll makes lies purely in their external appearance, which unfortunately may soon deteriorate or when the dolls are very expensive they will be guarded by Argus eye mother or governess. Mr. Max Brethfeld wrote the following in an article concerning the past Fall Fair: 'Such a doll is an educational nonsense because a doll should not be a snobbish fashionable lady but rather a small child.'

"Little children are indeed what the doll reform is all about, dear awkward children faces with questioning eyes, bashful smile, blonde or brown funzy hair or nicely plaited pigtails, in short a thoroughly artistic creation and understanding of children." (From the review of *Toys, Jewelry and Sports Article*, 1910.)

"Although the success of the given company (meaning Kämmer & Reinhardt) with their character dolls was so

Freddy with series number 1428 (by Simon & Halbig, but without a company mark) is a very intensely modeled character child, especially around the eyes. In painting he resembles the dolls from Kämmer & Reinhardt series, which were later given glass sleep eyes, possibly made by the same artist. He came with baby or with jointed body, 11½in (29cm), circa 1914.

Babies were the dolls children loved the most. Here is "Bonnie Babe" originated by Georgine Averill. The pictured baby was made by Georg Borgfeldt, is numbered 1105/3652/5, has cloth body and is 19½in (50cm) high. Circa 1920s.

Small boy from Franz Schmidt & Co., baby body, 12½in (32cm) high, neck mark 1295, circa 1912.

A young gardener by Schoenhut, already with a wig, created around 1913. Old clothing, wooden jointed body, 16in (41cm)

enormous, nevertheless one has to acknowledge that this movement is already declining. In the last year less dolls were sold than in the previous year, and if one is not mistaken, the business will be even more reduced in this year.

"It seems to us that the main reason is that the children demand 'sleep eyes' in their dolls. The doll must be able to sleep. Naturally one can insert glass eyes in the character dolls — it is done quite often now, but experience has shown that a really characteristic doll head does not suffer insertion of sleep eyes. The features of the child assume a completely different expression when the eyes close, thus it happens that the face that appears childlike assumes an uncanny and unnatural caricature like look.

"But because the children demanded unconditionally sleep eyes in their dolls, some manufacturers, whose so called character heads were less realistic, achieved a great success last year with their character heads with sleep eyes. We mention only the firm J.D. Kestner Jr. in Waltershausen and Franz Schmidt & Co. in Georgenthal. Perhaps the Kämmer & Reinhardt Company did the right thing, since the artistically executed picture of their new doll 'My Sweet Darling' in this issue is very effective and exceedingly sweet.

The new head with sleep eyes and eyelashes is a happy medium between a character head and the old style head. It is not, as the picture clearly shows, as inexpressive as the old heads and it is nevertheless beautiful." (One speaks here of the series number 121.)(From the *Wegweiser fur die Spiel-, Galanterie- und Kurzwaren-Industrie*, 1912.)

"The character dolls were a great mistake of the artists and the manufacturers. The public rejected them immediately with a startling unanimity and today they disappeared completely from the scene. They achieved a limited existence only because their realistic character was modified so that they resembled more and more the old doll heads. Approximately half, occasionally even three quarters or more of all dolls sold today were recruited from these 'beautified' babies with sleep eyes,

The doll reform began with the artist dolls from the group of Marion Kaulitz. Munich artist doll with composition wood head, painted eyes and open-closed smiling mouth, original dress, 19½in (50cm), circa 1908.

curls and smiling mouth. The other part of the realm was upheld by the unchanged good old dolls. They won a complete victory. The ladies desired beautiful dolls and the children were always attracted to them!" (From Erich Wulf in *Berliner Tagblatt*, January 25, 1914.)

I want to thank with all my heart the following collectors, who trusted me with their treasures in my adventurous and in part harassing photographic undertaking: Dr. Ansarian, Gabrielle von Eicken, Katharina Engels (Rothenburg Doll Museum), Ursula Gauder-Bonnet, Ella Haas, Ulricke Heuss, Mrs. Karl, Katja Kempkens, Liz Koerle, Mrs. Kursell, Elisabeth Otremba, Karin Schmelker, Mrs. Schmelcher, Vicki Schweizer, Paul and Gertrud Stuhlmuller, Marlies Tabizel, Countess Maree Tarnowska, Hildegard Trienekens, Mrs. Umbreit, Horst and Ute Weber.

I thank the family Ulbricht, Richard Wright and his photographer Anne Jackson and Mrs. Lauber and her photographer Helmut Lawrinenko for photographs. I especially appreciate their heartwarming readiness and complete support of my requests although they did not know me personally.

Back cover of the book: The 117n comes with normal glass sleep eyes as well as with flirting eyes. This one can really flirt! She is waiting under a Marklin street lantern. Surprisingly this one is marked with 117x, not with "n" as would correspond to the type of the model. A "x" was formerly used for dolls with short wooly hair glued to the crown of a closed head ("flocked hair"). Jointed body, 13¾in (35cm) high, circa 1916.

Books for Collectors from Germany

The beauty and detail of the color photographs is the international language of collectors. Text is in the German language.

Sabine Reinelt   **Kathe Kruse-Leben und Work (Her Life and Work)**
Ursula Brecht   **Kostbare Puppen (Precious Dolls)**
Catharina von Eijk-Prasing   **Puppen sammeln (Collecting Dolls)**   Item #3919
Sabine Reinelt   **Puppen und Spielzeug aus Zelluloid (Celluloid Dolls and Toys)**   Item #3794
Marion Forek-Schmahl   **Kunstobjeckt Puppe (Dolls As Art Objects)**   Item #4148
Kunz/Schneiders   **Schone alte Puppenstuben (Beautfiul Old Dollrooms)**   Item #3796
Sabine Reinelt   **Puppenkuche und Puppenherd (Dollhouse Kitchens and Stoves)**   Item #3797
Heinold/Rau   **Holzspielzeug aus aller Welt (Wooden Toys From Around the World)**   Item #3795
Rolf and Christel Pistorius   **Steiff-Sensational Teddy Bears, Animals & Dolls**, English language edition   Item #3982
Sabine Reinelt   **Zauber der Puppenwelt (The Enchanting World of Dolls)**   Item #4670
Rolf and Christel Pistorius   **Teddys Traumwelt**   Item #4669

All books available from Hobby House Press 1-800-554-1447

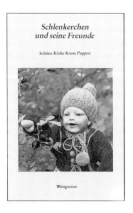

Postcard Books
Herzliche Puppengrusse   Item #4665
   12 Antique doll postcards
Schlenkerchen und seine Freunde   Item #4666
   12 Kathe Kruse doll postcards
Ein Gruss vom Teddy   Item #4667
   12 Antique Large Teddy Bears
Mit barigen Urlaubsgrussen   Item #4668
   12 Antique Steiff Teddy Bears